THE WEAPONS ENCYCLOPÆDIA

TANK AIRCRAFT AFV SHIP ARTILLERY VEHICLES SECRET WEAPON

 STURMGESCHÜTZ III Sd.Kfz. 142

THE WEAPONS ENCYCLOPAEDIA

EDITORIAL STAFF

Luca Cristini, Paolo Crippa.

ACADEMIC STAFF

Enrico Acerbi, Massimiliano Afiero, Aldo Antonicelli, Ruggero Calò, Luigi Carretta, Flavio Chistè, Anna Cristini, Carlo Cucut, Salvo Fagone, Enrico Finazzer, Arturo Giusti, Björn Huber, Andrea Lombardi, Aymeric Lopez, Marco Lucchetti, Gabriele Malavoglia, Luigi Manes, Giovanni Maressi, Francesco Mattesini, Daniele Notaro, Péter Mujzer, Federico Peirani, Alberto Peruffo, Maurizio Raggi, Andrea Alberto Tallillo, Antonio Tallillo, Massimo Zorza.

PUBLISHED BY

Luca Cristini Editore (Soldiershop), via Orio, 35/4 - 24050 Zanica (BG) ITALY.

DISTRIBUTION BY

Soldiershop - www.soldiershop.com, Amazon, Ingram Spark, Berliner Zinnfigurem (D), LaFeltrinelli, Mondadori, Libera Editorial (Spain), Google book (eBook), Kobo, (eBoook), Apple Book (eBook).

PUBLISHING'S NOTES

None of unpublished images or text of our book may be reproduced in any format without the expressed written permission of Luca Cristini Editore (already Soldiershop.com) when not indicate as marked with license creative commons 3.0 or 4.0. Luca Cristini Editore has made every reasonable effort to locate, contact and acknowledge rights holders and to correctly apply terms and conditions to Content. Every effort has been made to trace the copyright of all the photographs. If there are unintentional omissions, please contact the publisher in writing at: info@soldiershop.com, who will correct all subsequent editions.

LICENSES COMMONS

This book may utilize part of material marked with license creative commons 3.0 or 4.0 (CC BY 4.0), (CC BY-ND 4.0), (CC BY-SA 4.0) or (CC0 1.0). We give appropriate attribution credit and indicate if change were made in the acknowledgments field. Our WTW books series utilize only fonts licensed under the SIL Open Font License or other free use license.

CONTRIBUTORS OF THIS VOLUME & ACKNOWLEDGEMENTS

Ringraziamo i principali collaboratori di questo numero: I profili dei carri sono tutti dell'autore. Le colorazioni delle foto sono di Anna Cristini. Ringraziamenti particolari a istituzioni nazionali e/o private quali: Stato Maggiore dell'esercito, Archivio di Stato, Bundesarchiv, Nara, Library of Congress, Wikipedia, USAF, Signal magazine, Cronache di guerra, Fronte di guerra, IWM, Australian War Museum, ecc. A P.Crippa, A.Lopez, L.Manes, Péter Mujzer, C.Cucut, archivi Tallillo. Model Victoria (www.modelvictoria.it) ecc. per avere messo a disposizione immagini o altro dei loro archivi.

For a complete list of Soldiershop titles, or for every information please contact us on our website: www.soldiershop.com or www.cristinieditore.com. E-mail: info@soldiershop.com. Keep up to date on Facebook https://www.facebook.com/soldiershop.publishing

Title: **STUG III SD.KFZ. 142** Code.: **TWE-021 EN**
Series by L. S. Cristini
ISBN code: 9791255890881 first edition April 2024
THE WEAPONS ENCYCLOPAEDIA (SOLDIERSHOP) is a trademark of Luca Cristini Editore

STUG III
Sd.Kfz. 142

LUCA STEFANO CRISTINI

BOOK SERIES FOR MODELERS & COLLECTORS

CONTENTS

▲ StuG III Ausf. B which in April 1942 took part in the first day of the Fall Blau offensive in the area allocated to the Hungarian 2nd Army stationed between Kursk and Voronezh. Private collection.

INTRODUCTION

The **Sturmgeschütz III**, almost always shortened to **StuG III**, was a formidable assault gun supplied to the German Army during World War II, carved from the hull of the Panzer III medium tank from which it borrowed the entire rolling train, tracks, etc. The installation of the main armament was arranged in a rigid casemate instead of a revolving turret. This certainly reduced the capabilities of the vehicle, even though it was a self-propelled artillery gun (but increasingly also an anti-tank version); nevertheless the vehicle was easier to produce and cheaper, so much so that it became the Wehrmacht's trump card. The idea of the assault gun was conceived by the famous General von Manstein as early as 1935 as a support in providing close artillery support to infantry units for the elimination of enemy defensive obstacles such as machine gun nests, bunkers, counter-tank guns, etc.), so originally the Sturmgeschütz were not intended to engage tanks. In the course of the war, however, the tactical employment of the Sturmgeschütz was changed, and since 1942, given their technical characteristics and field trials, they were employed as tank fighters in addition to infantry support, leaving the original task of infantry support to the Sturmhaubitze 42. In the last months of the war, also due to the shortage of vehicles, they were even tactically used as tanks. It was so successful that it was the most produced tracked armoured fighting vehicle and the second most produced German armoured fighting vehicle (especially the Type IIIG) of any type after the half-track Sd.Kfz. 25. As many as 9,400 examples were produced!

▲ Early StuG III tank with the typical 75mm short-barreled cannon. We are in Russia immediately after the start of Operation Barbarossa at an SS unit. Bundesarchiv (author's colouring).

▲ ▼ StuG III Ausf. D captured by the British and photographed. Wikipedia.

DEVELOPMENT

Already in the final part of the First World War, the Germans had guessed that armoured support would be needed to assault fortifications. Following the development of the tactical concept of employing artillery as close support for the infantry, on the main intuition of General von Manstein, he presented a plan to Army Chief von Beck as early as 1935. In June 1936, Daimler-Benz finally received the order for the study, development and production of an infantry support vehicle armed with a 75 mm gun. The specifications stipulated that the calibre should be 7.5 cm, with a maximum range of at least 6 kilometres, and in any case be equipped with armament to ensure infantry support and as a secondary function as a tank destroyer; it had to be mounted in a rigid casemate that allowed considerable savings in the cost of the vehicle, being equipped with good armour and had a particularly low profile (it had to be no taller than an average height soldier). Daimler-Benz took all these requirements into account and used the hull, suspension and rolling train of the widespread and robust Panzer III Ausf.

STUG III AUSF B ASSAULT GUN, RUSSIA, WINTER 1941-42

▲ StuG.III Ausf.B, unidentified unit, Russian Front, winter 1941-1942, in classic white camouflage.

▲ StuG assault gun assembly line. The main factories involved in the production were Damler Benz, Alkett and MIAG. Bundesarchiv (author's colouring).

The first StuGs were equipped with a short-barreled, 7.5-cm Krupp StuK 37 L/24 cannon, which looked very similar to a howitzer. This type of barrel characterised the entire production run from the A to the D model. Its unique function meant that for a while, the General Staff did not know whether to consider the vehicle as an artillery, infantry or armoured force vehicle. In fact, this attribution ended up having only theoretical value. The units were assigned to the artillery, divided into battalions, with the main and only purpose of supporting the infantry, in time their strong value as anti-tank vehicles was discovered and they ended up being used in that branch as well. It was precisely the transition from short to long guns that allowed the StuG's special tank hunting capabilities to be discovered! In fact, in Russia, StuGs with short guns could not adequately engage Russian vehicles such as the KV-1 and T-34. Things changed with the adoption of the StuG G, which was equipped with a 7.5 cm StuK 40 L/43 high-speed gun (spring 1942) and later in the autumn of 1942 with a slightly longer 7.5 cm StuK 40 L/48 gun, i.e. the same guns mounted on the Panzer IV. These guns were less effective in removing infantry obstacles, but were of unparalleled effectiveness in knocking out enemy tanks. Returning to the economic advantages, the StuG costed 1/5 less than a Panzer III due to the fixed casemate turret about RM 80,000 instead of RM 103,000!

TECHNICAL FEATURES

The StuG III used the hull, rolling train and motorisation of the super-tested Panzer III, the upper part where the turret ring was located was replaced by a casemate in which the main armament was housed, initially a StuK L/24 75 mm cannon (the gun tube would be classified as a howitzer and not a cannon). In the first version, the vehicle was devoid of secondary armament. Then, from the spring of 1942, a first,

STURMGESCHÜTZ III Sd.Kfz. 142

7.92 mm MG34 machine gun was added, which could be mounted on a shield above the superstructure for greater anti-infantry protection. A second 7.92 mm coaxial MG34 began to appear in 1944 and became standard on all production during the same year. The casemate that defined the lines of the StuG was as short and wide as the vehicle. The width then increased further due to the massive use of Schürzen (a kind of spaced armoured side reinforcements/ skirts), which were also widely used on many panzers. At the front was a large opening to accommodate the bulky main gun structure. On top were two-piece hatches for the pilot in the front, two large two-piece hatches for the crew in the rear casemate and an open space to the left for the commander's periscope. The engine could be accessed through several large hatches on the rear deck of the vehicle. The pilot had a reinforced visual slit and a binocular sight to help with manoeuvres. During the evolution of the StuG, the shape of the casemate changed significantly from the F and especially G versions, and adopted two types of mounts, the normal one on the Ausf. F and the so-called 'pig-nose' one for the largely revised Ausf. G extensively revised, which helps to distinguish between the two models. The crew of four (pilot, commander, gunner and loader) all housed in the casemate. The general arrangements inside were those of the Panzer III, with the engine at the rear and the transmission components at the front (in front of the fighting compartment). From the first version, the armour chosen was fairly thick (50mm).

▲ Further details of the StuG III D Sturmgescühtz Russia, August-September 1943. Wikipedia.

STUG III AUSF C/D ASSAULT GUN, RUSSIA 1943

▲ StuG. III Ausf.C/D, belonging to the 192nd Sturmgeschütz-Abteilung. Russian Front, 1941.

ARMAMENT

The main weapon of the early StuGs was, as already mentioned, the 7.5 cm L/24 (24-calibre) Krupp gun. This was essentially a short-barreled howitzer adapted to fire HE projectiles, which were particularly effective against enemy fortifications and positions. It was an adaptation of the 7.5 cm KwK L/24 tank gun originally designed for the Panzer IV. It was highly suitable for launching attacks and destroying forts and bunkers at various distances. The 7.5-cm Kampfwagenkanone-37 L/24 was equipped with a wide and varied array of different types of ammunition during the war, eventually becoming a very specialised vehicle for destroying anti-infantry obstacles. The normal supply was about fifty rounds of the various types on board the vehicle. From the F and G versions, with the adoption of the longer Stu.K. L/40 version, the penetration capacity of the projectiles (especially useful for anti-tank activities) was greatly improved These projectiles were bulkier and larger, consequently, the total load dropped to 44 payloads. Initially, the vehicle had no other armament, then a first MG was added, and later a second machine gun. Initially, the tank relied exclusively on accompanying infantry for close-range defence, which also had a rationale for the tactical use to which it was assigned. From the upgraded G version (December 1942), an initial Maschinengewehr 34 protected by a shield was mounted. The personal weapons available to the crew generally included an MP 38 light machine gun and several P 38 automatic weapons. In order to obtain maximum yield from the cannon fire, indirect aiming was used, which, however, acted to the detriment of accuracy. Below 500 metres, precision shooting was preferably pursued. To achieve good results, the quality of the on-board optical instrumentation proved crucial. As early as the Ausf. C, D and E a new ZF1 sight was introduced, with a reticle pattern comprising seven triangles separated by four mils, which was particularly effective. However, the lack of a rotating turret forced the vehicle to move constantly, especially when targeting moving targets. The distance between the triangles was used to aim at moving targets.

ENGINE

The engine was the reliable and proven series-produced Maybach HL 120 TRM V-12 petrol engine, which delivered around 300 hp (296 bhp or 221 kW) and a power-to-weight ratio of 12.6 hp/tonne, connected to a six-speed transmission. The wheel train comprised six tyred wheels coupled on torsion arms and three double return rollers per side. The sprocket wheels were at the front, while the tensioning wheels were at the rear. The tracks were made of mild steel and identical to the Panzer III model.

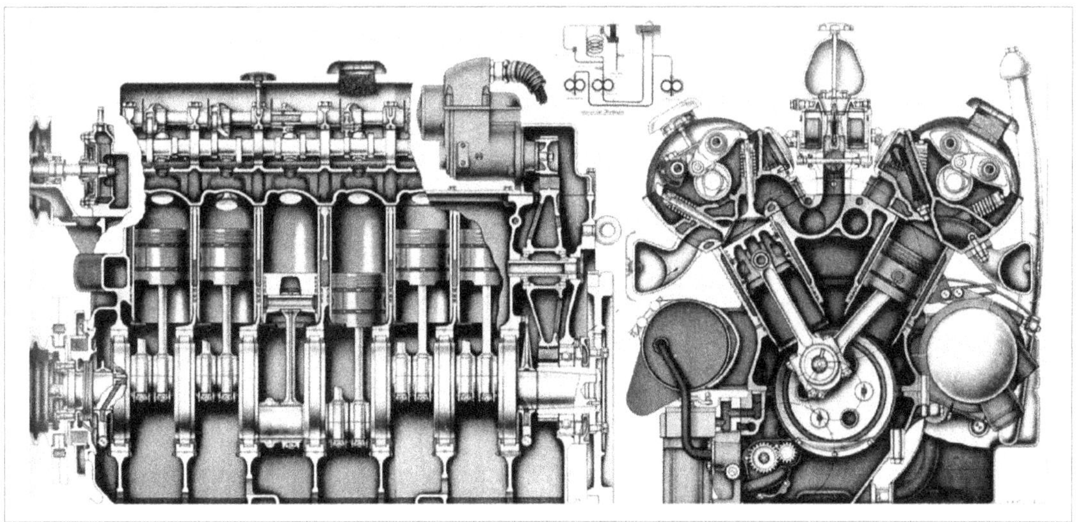

▲ View of the engine of the StuG III, the Maybach HL 120. Wikipedia.

STUG III AUSF. D ASSAULT GUN, NORTH AFRICA 1942

▲ StuG.III Ausf.D belonging to Sonderverband 288, Deutsche Afrika Korps, North Africa 1942.

▲ Sturmgeschütz StuG III Ausf C/D supporting infantry, engaged in the Battle of Stalingrad in 1942. Bundesarchiv, colouring of the author.

◄ A StuG III G in wait in the Russian campaign,1942. Bundesarchiv.

▼ Artillerymen intent on loading the ammunition of a StuG III G in a Russian village in 1942. Bundesarchiv.

STUG III AUSF E ASSAULT GUN, RUSSIA, AUTUMN 1942

▲ StuG.III Ausf.E belonging to an unidentified unit, Russian Front, autumn 1942.

VERSIONS OF THE VEHICLE

There were numerous versions of the StuG III between pre-series and officers, from A to G, for 8 different models; some variants also for assault guns and flamethrowers. The Stug III models were the Ausf. A, B, C, D, E, F, F/8 and G (where Ausf. is an abbreviation for *Ausführung*, meaning 'model' or 'version' in German). The first versions were all produced by Daimler-Benz, later joined by Alkett and finally MIAG.

StuG III prototypes (1937, these were five vehicles mounted on Panzer III Ausf. B chassis): in December 1937, two vehicles were in service with the 1st Panzer Regiment in Erfurt. The vehicles had eight wheels on each side with 360 millimetre (14 inch) wide tracks, a 14.5 mm thick soft steel superstructure and the 7.5 cm StuK 37 L/24 cannon. Although not suitable for combat, they were then used for training purposes until 1941.

StuG III Ausf. A (Sd.Kfz. 142; 36 examples built in January-May 1940, produced by Daimler-Benz). First used in the Battle of France, the StuG III Ausf. A used a modified 5. /ZW chassis (Panzer III Ausf. F) with front armour reinforced to 50 mm. The last six vehicles of the 36 built were built on chassis derived from the Panzer III Ausf. G production.

StuG III Ausf. B: (Sd.Kfz 142; 300 examples produced June 1940-May 1941, from Alkett) Chassis 7. /ZW modified (Panzer III Ausf. H), track widened (380 mm). Consequently, two rubber tyres on each wheel were widened by 16 mm each. Both wheel types were interchangeable. The annoying 10-speed transmission of the A model was replaced with a more practical 6-speed. On the whole, the B version underwent a series of improvements and innovations in the rolling train, tracks, drive wheels etc.

▲ A StuG III Ausf.B in a Russian village in 1941. Bundesarchiv (author colouring).

StuG III Ausf. C: (Sd.Kfz 142; 50 examples produced in April 1941, also by Alkett). The gunner's view window, which had proved deadly for the gunner, was removed; instead, accommodation for the gunner's periscope was made at the top of the superstructure. The rear idler wheel was redesigned.

StuG III Ausf. D: (Sd.Kfz 142; 150 examples produced by Aklett in May-September 1941). Vehicle substantially similar to the C version. Only new features: On-board intercom installed, new transmission hatch locks added.

StuG III Ausf. E: (Sd.Kfz 142; 284 examples produced in the period: September 1941 - February 1942) Extensive rectangular armoured boxes were added to the sides of the superstructure to house the radio equipment, allowing for more interior space. An MG 34 made its first appearance to protect the vehicle from enemy infantry. Vehicle commanders were officially provided with the new SF14Z stereoscopic scissor periscopes.

StuG III Ausf. F: (Sd.Kfz 142/1; 366 examples produced in the period: March-September 1942). Starting with the F series, the short barrel was retired, this version used the longer 7.5 cm StuK 40 L/43 gun. This gun allowed the Ausf. F to finally be able to engage most Soviet armoured vehicles at normal combat distances. This radical modification, in effect, mutated a substantial tactical change in the use of the StuG, which had become more of a tank fighter than an infantry support vehicle. The Schürzen were reinforced and 30mm armour plates were added to the 50mm front armour from June 1942, so that the front armour was a full 80mm stronger. From June 1942, the Ausf. F was fitted with a new StuK 40 L/48 gun that was 7.5 cm longer than its predecessor. This weapon was even more powerful in terms of penetrating enemy armour.

StuG III Ausf. F/8: (Sd.Kfz 142/1; 250 examples produced in the period: September-December 1942for a total of 616 Ausf F) Introduction of an improved hull design similar to that already used for the Panzer III Ausf. J/L with increased rear armour. This was the eighth version of the Panzer III hull, hence the designation 'F/8'. From the F/8 version, the 7.5 cm StuK 40 L/48 gun became the standard until the last of the Ausf. G.

▲ Column of StuG III Ausf.B engaged in the first operations of the invasion of the Soviet Union in 1941. Bundesarchiv (author's colouring).

ASSAULT GUN STUIG-33B, RUSSIA, STALINGRAD 1942

▲ German Sturm-Infanteriegeschütz 33B equipped with the 15 cm sIG 33 howitzer for close infantry support, Stalingrad, autumn 1942. A total of 12 of the 24 converted vehicles were deployed on this front

StuG III Ausf. G (Sd.Kfz. 142/1; 8,423 examples produced in the period: December 1942 - April 1945): the last and by far the most common of the StuG series. The upper superstructure appears here still enlarged: the famous armoured boxes on both sides were suppressed. This new superstructure design made the StuG the tallest of the series at up to 2160 mm. From March 1943, the pilot's periscope was also suppressed. In February 1943, Aklett was joined by the MIAG factory as the second manufacturer. From May 1943, spaced armour plates on the side hulls *(Schürzen) were* also fitted to the G models; these were mainly intended for protection against Russian anti-tank guns, but were also useful against hollow charge ammunition. The *Schürzen* were later added to some Ausf. F/8 models, ahead of and in preparation for the Battle of Kursk. However, the mounts for the *Schürzen* proved to be not without flaws, as many were lost on the battlefield. From March 1944, an improved mounting system was then introduced; as a result, side skirts became increasingly standard with the last Ausf G model. From May 1943, 80 mm thick plates were used for the front armour instead of the two 50 mm + 30 mm plates already specified. A new rotating dome with periscopes was added for the Ausf G commander. However, from September 1943, the chronic lack of ball bearings (due to the USAAF bombing of the Schweinfurt factories) forced the welding of the domes. The newly available ball bearings were installed again from August 1944. From December 1942, a square protective shield was installed for the machine gun and magazine, making it possible for the first time to install an MG34 directly at the factory on a StuG. The F/8 models, on the other hand, had adapted machine gun defence shields from early 1943. From October 1943, the G versions were fitted with the *Topfblende* gun shroud *(often called Saukopf* 'pig's head') without a coaxial mount. This cast shroud, which had a sloping, rounded shape, was more effective in deflecting shots than the original square *Kastenblende shroud,* which had armour thicknesses ranging from 45 mm to 50 mm. The lack of large castings meant that the trapezoid-shaped squared mantle was also produced until the end. Topfblende were almost exclusively mounted on vehicles produced by Alkett and not MIAG. A new coaxial machine gun was added first to the squared cloaks, from June 1944, and then to the Topfblende cloak, from October 1944. With the addition of this coaxial machine gun, all StuGs were now equipped with two MG 34 machine guns. Some StuGs previously fitted with a square shroud had a coaxial machine gun hole drilled to fit a coaxial machine gun. Finally, the Zimmerit antimagnetic coating to protect the vehicles from magnetic mines was applied starting in September (at MIAG) or November (at Alkett) 1943 and ending in September 1944.

OTHER VARIANTS

StuH 42 (Sd.Kfz 142/2 1,300 examples produced in the Aklett period from March 1943 to March 1945). In 1942, a variant of the StuG Ausf. F was designed with a real 4.1-inch (10.5 cm) howitzer instead of the 7.5-cm StuK 40 L/43 gun. These new vehicles were designated **StuH 42** (*Sturmhaubitze 42*, Sd.Kfz 142/2). The purpose of these new vehicles was to be able to continue providing infantry support, leaving the StuG F and especially G with their new function as anti-tank vehicles. The StuH 42 mounted a variant of the 10.5 cm LeFH 18 howitzer, modified to be electrically operated and equipped with a muzzle brake. Models were produced from the StuG III Ausf. G. The muzzle brake in this case was avoided due to lack of resources during the war. Alkett produced 1,300 StuH 42s from March 1943 to 1945.

StuG III (Flamm) During 1943, 10 StuG IIIs were converted to the **StuG III (Flamm)** configuration by replacing the main gun with a Schwade flamethrower. These vehicles were all converted for the purpose. To date, their combat use is unknown.

StuIG 33B or **Sturminfanteriegeschütz 33B**, was a German assault gun employed during World War II. It was also derived from the Sturmgeschütz III assault gun and was armed with a 150 mm howitzer in a

STUG III AUSF F ASSAULT GUN, RUSSIA 1942

▲ StuG.III Ausf.F, belonging to the 191st Sturmgeschütz-Abteilung. Russian Front, 1942.

▲ The German crew of a StuG III Ausf B with a short barrel, bearing the numerous victories against opposing tanks, engaged in the crossing of the Desan River during the first (successful) eastward phase of Operation Barbarossa in 1941. Bundesarchiv. Small photo: a Stug in a Russian village.

STUG III AUSF G ASSAULT GUN, RUSSIA, LATE 1944

▲ StuG.III Ausf.G, unidentified unit, Russian Front, late 1944. In February 1943, the basic colour was changed to Dunkelgelb RAL 7028. A camouflage pattern could be added to this colour using two colours Olive grün RAL 6003 and Rotbraun 8017. In the case of this assault gun, it appears that only a winter white coat was applied over the base colour. The number 02 in red is clearly visible on the turret next to the balkenkreuz.

heavily armoured quadrangular casemate, in order to closely support the operations of infantry divisions. It proved to be a coarse and elephantine vehicle and tended to break down often. Nevertheless, it proved itself in battle, and the General Staff did not abandon the assault cannon concept while studying more suitable means. Twenty-four StuIG 33Bs were produced, all based on the old StuG III chassis, of which twelve vehicles took part in the Battle of Stalingrad where they were destroyed or captured. The remaining 12 vehicles were assigned to the 23rd Panzer Division.

▲ Occupation of Grodno by German troops. Loading ammunition into the StuG III Ausf E assault gun. Wikipedia CC3.

▲► Sturmgeschütz StuG III Ausf C/D engaged in the Battle of Stalingrad in 1942. Bundesarchiv, author's colouring.

STURMGESCHÜTZ III Sd.Kfz. 142

OPERATIONAL USE

OPERATIONAL HISTORY OF STUGS III

With its low profile, aggressive features and low cost, the StuG was the Wehrmacht's true workhorse, transforming itself from a close support vehicle to a premier tank fighter, it fought non-stop, everywhere from North Africa to Europe and Russia. The crews loved it for its low profile and good armour, and the infantry it supported were grateful for its firepower and availability. The StuG were deadly snipers in the defence of the Reich from 1943 to 1945. The StuG took out more enemy tanks than the Panzers and Tigers combined. In 1944 alone they destroyed over 20,000 armoured vehicles. The Sturmgeschütz crews were gunners, but they considered themselves elite, and propaganda newsreels extolled them on a par with submariners and Luftwaffe aces! Due to its versatility and economy, the StuG was used on every single front the Wehrmacht was engaged on, from the coasts of France and Norway to the Volga in the east, and in Africa, from the gates of Egypt to the hills of Tunisia, and was also widely distributed to all of Germany's allies. Because of their low silhouette, the StuG IIIs were easy to camouflage and conceal and were very difficult targets to destroy. By the end of the war, over 11,300 StuG IIIs and StuH 42s had been built, but by April 1945, the tally showed huge losses, leaving a German residue of only 1,053 StuG IIIs and 277 StuH 42s.

THE RUSSIAN CAMPAIGN

At the start of Operation Barbarossa, in its first 15 days of operation, a single StuG unit destroyed almost 100 Russian tanks and captured 23, destroyed 23 bunkers, ten armoured trains and interrupted convoys, destroying vehicles of all kinds everywhere. It was customary for the StuGs to identify distant targets first, thanks to the improved optical instruments with which they were equipped, the infantry supported their shooting and sniping by providing close visual coverage to the side and rear.

In direct tank combat, the StuG III in this early phase of the conflict with the Soviets proved superior to any Soviet tank encountered (T-26 and BT-5/7 for the most part but also some KV-1s). Above all, it was the thermal discomfort and adverse weather conditions that were the real enemy of the StuGs that year; many failures occurred even before it got really cold, especially affecting the transmissions. With the winter, things got worse as snow mixed with mud and gravel, freezing every night. The crews were exhAusfed from working to keep their vehicles efficient. The StuGs fared no better than the other Panzers, sharing the same failures of mechanical parts on the chassis and tracks. The Russian winter was the real killer of the German Panzers and StuGs. This slaughter of vehicles by mechanical causes was no longer happening in the south where the other StuG Abteilung, even those equipped with short barrels like the StuG Ausf.A-E managed to destroy more T-34s than the Russian tanks did with the same StuGs. But already the first long-barreled StuG F was arriving at the front.... Krupp started work on the Pak L/42 cannon as early as January 1940, and the project developed until March 1941. It was soon enough clear to everyone that the long-barreled gun had to have a higher initial speed. Tests and studies were carried out, the result was the 40 7.5 cm L/43 cannon. A removable double-chamber muzzle brake with four side ports was added to reduce recoil. The Sturmgeschütz-Abteilung GrossDeutschland received a couple of dozen of the new Ausf.F 22 vehicles in March-April 1942. By the beginning of the summer offensive on the Eastern Front, there were already about 210 Ausf.F at the front. In November 1942, still 448 Ausf.F/G entered service with 22 units. During the recapture of Kharkov in February 1943, StuG units of the GrossDeutschland Division claimed the destruction of almost 50 T-34s (while the Tigers destroyed only 30). Around Leningrad, the StuGs did even better, knocking out 230 T-34s and KV-1s, suffering only 13 losses. Before Zitadelle, 727 StuG III Gs were already operating. German military reports clearly showed that the StuGs fared very well (especially when compared to the poor performance of the Tiger and various Panzers)), achieving the best combat performance for any given German armoured vehicle. Russian tank crews feared the StuG more than anything else and where they could they avoided combat against it. Casualties on the other

▲ In Russia, in order to counter the effectiveness of the anti-tank guns, armoured side reinforcements, a sort of mini-skirt called Shurzen, were adopted, which served the purpose very well. Bundesarchiv, author's colouring.

STUG III AUSF G ASSAULT GUN, KURSK, RUSSIA 1943

▲ Stug III Ausf.G assault gun belonging to the Panzer Grenadier Division Totenkopf in Kursk, Russia 1943.

▲ ▼ The commander of a StuG inside the combat chamber, observing the situation with his periscope. Below: The interior of the same view in a StuG preserved in a Spanish museum, from the photo you can appreciate the good internal organisation.

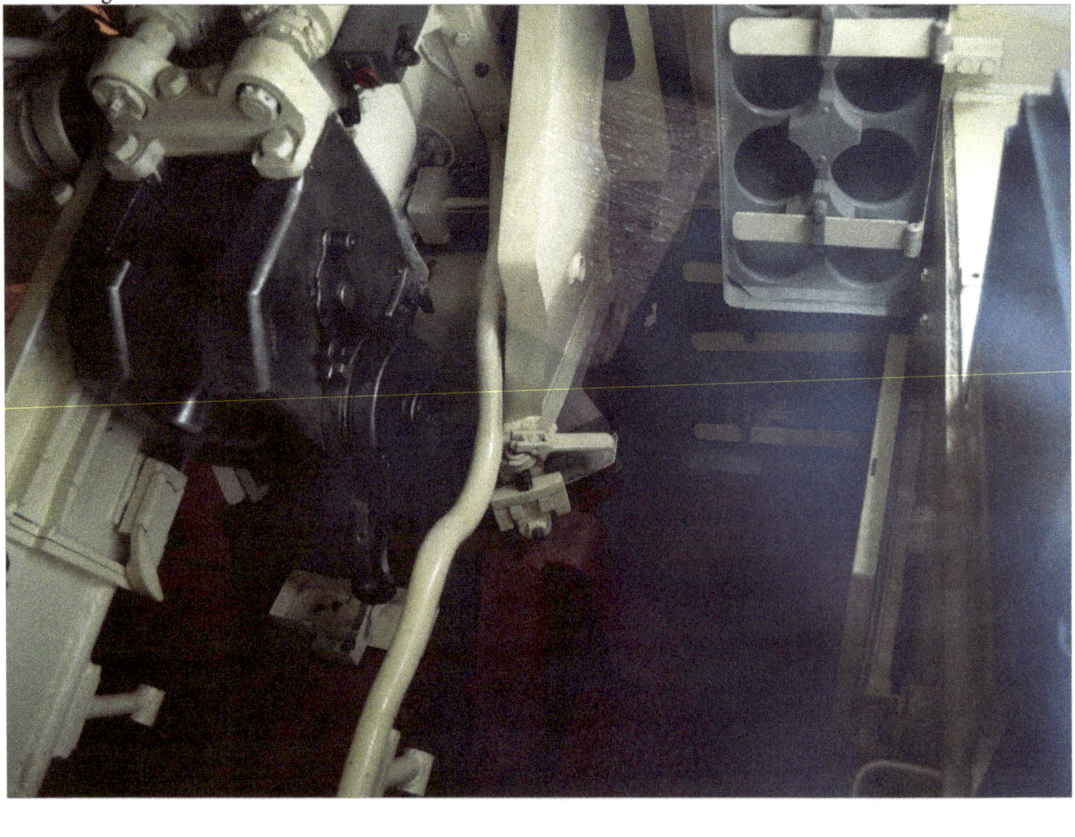

STURMGESCHÜTZ III Sd.Kfz. 142

STUG III AUSF G ASSAULT GUN, RUSSIA, LATE 1943

▲ StuG.III Ausf.G, of the 23ʳᵈ Sturmgeschütz Brigade, active on the Russian Front in late 1943.

hand were often the work of mines and the deadly Soviet anti-tank guns, which often managed to pierce the commander's dome. The Panzers, however, suffered far more from these things, with taller silhouettes and a far less refined optical system than the StuGs, the tank men envied their assault gun counterparts. In August 1943, 11 StuG battalions suffered 430 casualties against the loss of only eight vehicles. Much credit for the success was also given to the Schürzen side skirts, which saved their crews from the deadly anti-tank guns. At the same time in perfect counter-information style to confuse the enemy, the battalions were renamed into brigades. The huge Russian plains with no natural obstacles in between favoured the German vehicles that had more advanced radio systems. All these factors together with the tactical reorganisation resulted in high efficiency among the now highly experienced StuG units and great versatility against both infantry and opposing tanks. In December 1943, another report from the front stated that the chances of success increased significantly by using StuGs together with Panzer IVs. The pros and cons of these two vehicles balanced each other well. The frontal attack offered by the StuGs with their low silhouette assisted the Panzer IVs, which, with their rotating turret, provided lateral cover. Acting in synergy, the StuGs were free to engage a large number of targets simultaneously, especially in the impassable terrain of the Russian steppes. In short, engaging in close collaboration with the Panzer grenadiers was the most effective way to deal with enemy infantry positions, both providing optimal, mutual protection that worked wonders. Defensively, the StuGs in Russia were also in their element. Thanks to their low profile, easy camouflage and excellent long-range aiming, they could inflict enormous damage on tanks from a distance without manoeuvring, and then retreat to safety. However, as time went on, the superiority of the Panzer IVs in the offensive became apparent. From October to December, two dozen Panzer IVs destroyed 136 enemy tanks, while 15 StuGs claimed only 75.

▲ Beautiful picture of a StuG III Ausf G carrying an infantry platoon. The vehicle was, in fact, created to support infantrymen in operations to remove enemy defensive structures. Bundesarchiv (author's colouring).

STUG III AUSF G ASSAULT GUN, RUSSIA 1943-1944

▲ StuG.III Ausf.G, unidentified unit, Russian Front, 1943-44.

▲ Interesting picture showing the insertion of the weapon system in the casemate of the Stug III Ausf G. Bundesarchiv (author's colouring).

STUG III AUSF G ASSAULT GUN, FINLAND 1944

▲ StuG.III Ausf.G, belonging to the Finnish Army Assault Brigade, Enso Finland, June 1944.

WAR IN NORTH AFRICA (1941-1943)

The StuGs, it is not clear why, were sent sparingly to North Africa, in contrast to other theatres of operation. Sonderverband 288 was assigned four StuG Ausf.D (short-barreled version) to fight in the Gazal campaign. Two were lost on the sea voyage, the remaining two took part in the Battle of El Alamein (2nd battle). One of the two saved himself by being captured later at the surrender in Tunis. Six more F/8s were then sent to Tunisia with the 1st Sturmgeschütz-Abt. 242 but again only four survived the crossing. These were assigned to the Fallschirm Ramcke Brigade and were all lost in May 1943.

NORMANDY, SUMMER 1944

Among the units that served in northern France was the StuG 341 Brigade, which fought at Brecey, Southern Avranches/Pontaubault in late July and Chartres in August. It had several Ausf.G and some StuH 42s. Several other Brigades took part in the operations with defensive effectiveness, helped, again, by their low profile and, of course, the configuration of the combat terrain.

CAMPAIGN OF ITALY

In Italy, the StuH 42 were used by the Luftwaffe Division 'Hermann Göring' in 1944, while the Ausf.G of the 15th Panzer Grenadier Division served in Sicily in the autumn of 1943 and in Italy in 1944. The Sturmgeschütz-Abteilung 107 was active with the XIII SS Corps, 1st Army, Army Group G in northern Italy in 1945. Sturmgeschütz-Abteilung 242 was transferred to Italy in May 1943 and based in Liguria in 1945. Sturmgeschütz-Batterie 247 was established in March 1943, operated in Italy then in Sardinia and Corsica. Formed in January 1944, the Sturmgeschütz-Abteilung 907 sent to Italy, fought at Anzio and Monte Cassino. In February 1945, it was based in Liguria. In January, another 'Italian' StuG unit, Sturmgeschütz-Abteilung 914, was also formed and sent to Verona, before being renamed Sturmgeschütz-Brigade 720. It remained in service with the 10th Army at the beginning of 1945, then moved to Liguria. An independent unit, the Fallschirm-Sturmgeschütz-Brigade Schmitz, was formed in Italy in January 1945 and served with the 1st Parachute Corps, 10th Army in Liguria. It was then known as Fallschirm-Sturmgeschütz-Brigade 210.

▲ A StuG III G camouflaged in the snow with its infantry platoon in Russia 1943. Bundesarchiv.

▲ ▼ Battle of Stalingrad, a Stug III D packed with soldiers overtakes some Russian prisoners on their way to captivity. Below, also in Russia an armoured column of Panther V led by a Stug III ausf G are awaiting orders for movement. Bundesarchiv. Author's colouring.

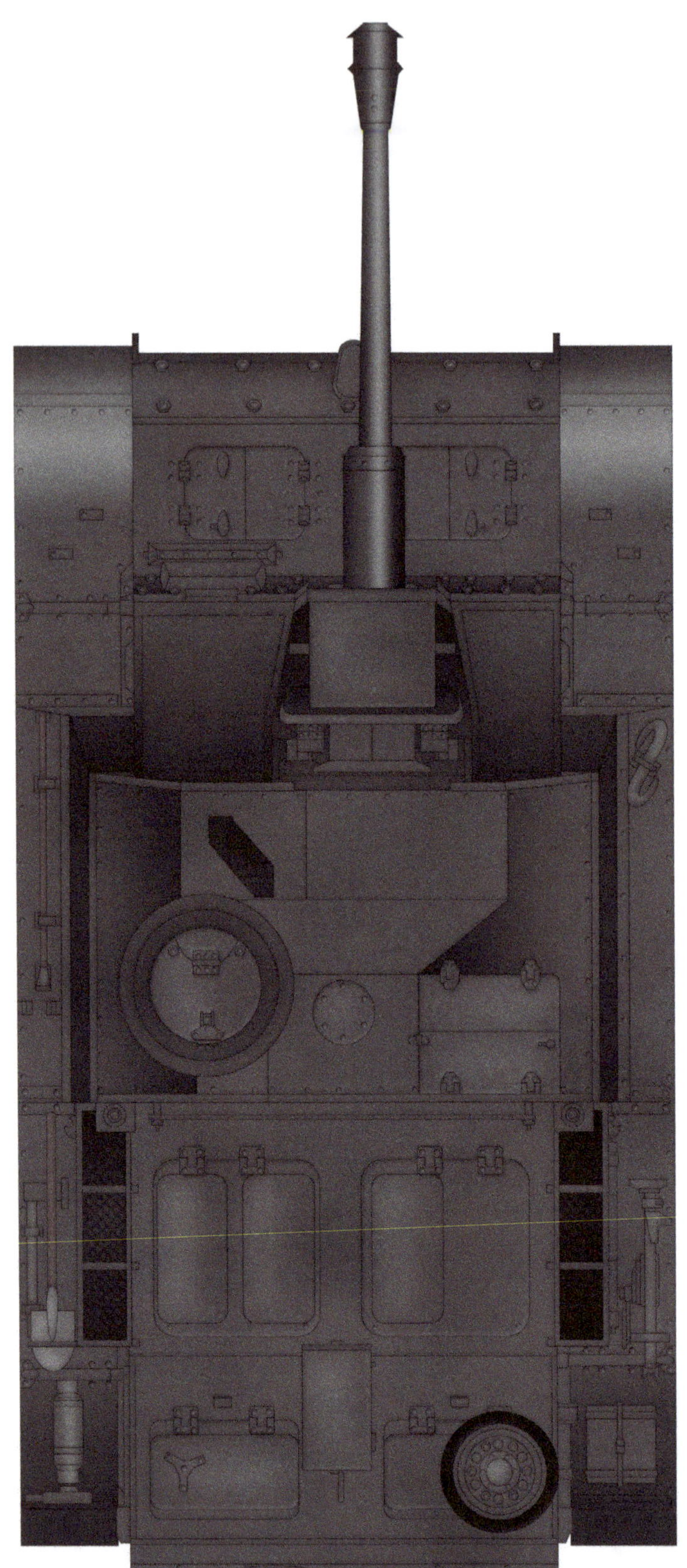

▲ Top view of the StuG III assault gun.

STUG III AUSF G ASSAULT GUN, RUSSIA 1944

▲ StuG.III Ausf.G, unidentified unit, active on the Belorussian Front, Russia 1944.

▲ A StuG III G lurking in the fields of the Ukraine during the Russian invasion. August 1942, Bundesarchiv (author's colouring). Below: the crew of a Stug in front of its operational vehicle in Russia, 1943. Bundesarchiv (author's colouring).

BULGARIAN ARMY STUG III AUSF G ASSAULT GUN, 1944

▲ StuG.III Ausf.G z of the 2nd Armoured Battalion of the Bulgarian Army at Plowdiw in Bulgaria, 1944.

▲ Front and rear view of the StuG III assault gun.

HUNGARIIAN ARMY STUG III AUSF G ASSAULT GUN - 1944

▲ StuG.Ill Aust.G z of the 7th Assault Gun of Hungarian Army August 1944. In the small photo shows a detail of the same destroyed vehicle. Mujzer Collection

▲ StuG.III Ausf.G, unidentified unit, Russian Front, 1944-45. At the end of 1944, the basic colour of all German AFVs changed to Olivegrün RAL 6003. The two remaining colours, Dunkelgelb RAL 7028 and Rotbraun 8017 were used for camouflage.

CAMOUFLAGE AND DISTINCTIVE SIGNS

In the early stages of the war in Poland and France, the German army mainly used vehicles painted in Dunkelgrau (RAL 7021), with some vehicles also painted in Dunkelbraun (RAL 7017) as a camouflage motif until the Oberkommando des Heeres decided that only Dunkelgrau should be used. The decision did not only apply to tanks, but also to all other vehicles or AFVs: armoured cars, half-tracks and even kitchen tanks were painted the same colour.

This Dunkelgrau is often shown in illustrations not too correctly. The point is that it is in reality a very dark bluish-grey colour. This erroneous fact is often due to the fact that grey tends to "blend" effectively with the surrounding colours and consequently appear much lighter.

The war fought, however, opened the eyes of Hitler's generals, especially in Russia and Africa. In both theatres of operation, Dunkelgrau could be seen miles away, a clear invitation to enemy fire. Therefore, the German divisions in the USSR used any useful material to colour their vehicles white, including natural materials such as chalk, sheets, piled snow and the inevitable whitewash. The resulting camouflage saved the skin of many a tank pilot....

These amateurish bleaches also had the advantage that they gradually washed away with the rains of late winter and early spring, melting like snow. The same problem in Libya, even though white was not needed here, a solution was found with typical German stubbornness and eventually a solution was found when Gelbbraun (RAL 8000) was assigned to that front and the vehicles in Dunkelgrau were quickly camouflaged with the desert. In addition to colouring in Gelbraun, Graugrün (RAL 7008) was also used in Africa, the latter in different variants conditioned by what the tank pilots had on hand, or what they managed to capture from the enemy.

Starting in 1942, official colours began to be in short supply at the front and often also at the factory. Military vehicles were therefore painted using copies or alternative colour schemes, especially for desert vehicles (more isolated than the homeland), using Braun (RAL 8020) and Grau (brown and grey, RAL 7027). On the pages of the book you will find a very clear mirror on these colours and the RAL designation.

In addition to Africa, vehicles painted in the two-tone camouflage already in use in the desert also began to be used on the Eastern Front. It must be remembered, however, that in mid-war most German tanks in Russia were still Dunkelgrau, at least until 1943, when the OKH issued a new order that the standard basic colour of all vehicles became Dunkelgelb (dark yellow, RAL 7028). The colour was not a true yellow, but rather tended towards bronze. A delicate colour, however, that varied, even enormously, depending on many factors: who painted it, how much it was diluted with solvents, time, wear and tear, etc. RAL 7028 offers, even in the bibliography, a large number of 'variants'!

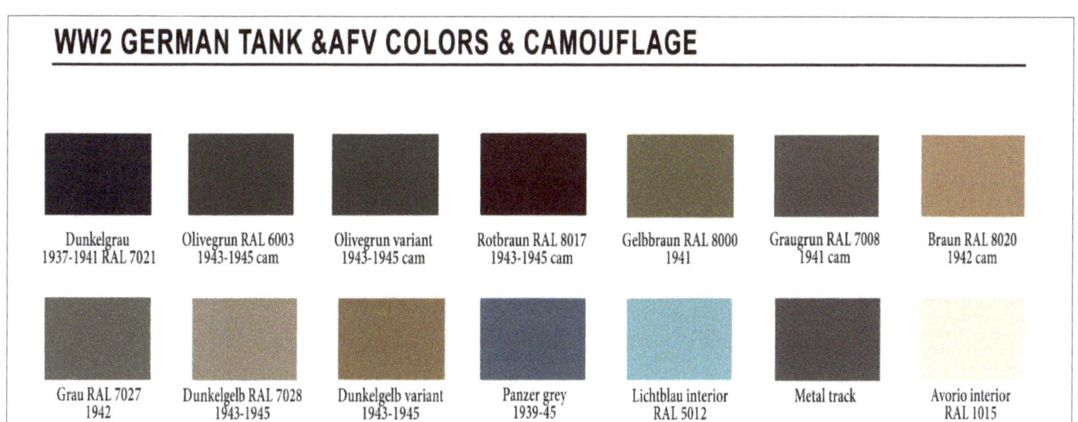

So it was partly by chance, partly by luck that they came up with the modern camouflage that the Germans called the *Hinterhalt-Tarnung* or '*Ambush*'. A complicated aspect to describe, but in fact it is an effect of light filtered through natural foliage, in short, a very effective camouflage. As with works of art, one could also speak of styles, as varied as possible. One was reminiscent of the *pointillisme* of the French Impressionists. A more 'orphic' one also called disc or mottled. The choice of one style or the other was also to a certain extent the signature of the factory that produced the vehicles (from mid-1944 the vehicles were painted in the production plants). The colours applied in the factory were a base of Dunkelgelb, with patches of Rotbraun (red brown) and Olivgrün (olive green). Storage problems, thunderstorms and other problems arose that made the outgoing supply varied.

Finally, in December 1944, a new order was issued that the tanks were to be painted all over with a base coat (over the red-oxide primer, the Italian minio) of Dunkelgrün and/or Olivgrün with applications of Dunkelgelb and Rotbraun stripes and stains, and this seems to be the last order given for camouflage while the war was in progress.

The application of camouflage was generally done with compressed-air paint sprays, failing which it was done 'the old-fashioned way': brushes, mops or simply rags on the end of a stick. These artifices, this art of contrivance ended up multiplying the camouflage variants that would later be destined for the battlefield.

Like all armies, the German army had realised (often before many) that concealing vehicles in defensive or offensive manoeuvres would increase the likelihood of surviving the clash. In addition to the camouflage painted on the vehicle itself, foliage (branches, bushes, hay, even stacks of wood) was therefore often used to cover the vehicle, usually from the front, to make it even more difficult to detect and distinguish from its surroundings. More rarely, tarpaulins and camouflage nets mixed with foliage were also used to further conceal the tank. Last but not least, mud and snow were also a cheap, but effective, camouflage that was very useful for blending in with the surroundings.

▲ Of course, the colouring and camouflage varied if the Stugs were operational in other armies, as in the case of this one in use in the Finnish army and preserved intact in the Paul Museum in Finland. Wikipedia Cc3.

STUG III AUSF G ASSAULT GUN, GERMANY, SPRING 1945

▲ StuG.III Ausf.G, a unit belonging to the 202nd Sturmgeschütz Brigade which, in the final part of the conflict, bore the serial number on the gun barrel. East German theatre of operations, spring 1945. Note the zimmerit on the turret.

▲ ▼ Italian campaign, above and below Stug III Ausf. G waiting to enter combat. The picture below shows the vehicle hiding near a huge prickly pear tree in Sicily. Italy 1943. Bundesarchiv (author's colouring).

▶ A StuG of Germanic forces crosses Via XX Settembre in Rome . Bundesarchiv.

STUG III AUSF G ASSAULT GUN, HUNGARY, JANUARY 1945

▲ StuG.III Ausf.G, belonging to SS-Panzerjäger-Abteilung 3, Szomor, Hungary, January 1945.

▲ A Stug III ausf G wagon mounted on the train to be sent to the front. Bundesarchiv (author's colouring).

▼ Alkett or MIAG factories where most versions of the StuG III G were produced. Interesting view of the assembly line. Bundesarchiv (author's colouring).

STURMGESCHÜTZ III Sd.Kfz. 142

PRODUCTION AND EXPORT

From 1936 onwards, after Daimler-Benz initiated the project, the German companies in charge of the construction of the StuG III in all its versions were mainly Alkett and MIAG: the production of all series models and its variants was over 10,000 units.

■ MAIN USERS

- **Nazi Germany**: was obviously the main operator, operating in practically all departments, even in the Luftwaffe in generally little-known units. The Sturmgeschütz-Abteilung 1 der Luftwaffe (formed in January 1944 for the I Fallschirm-Korps), operated near Nancy (eastern France) and in the Ardennes in the winter of 1944-45. Instead, the Sturmgeschütz-Abteilung 2 der Luftwaffe was formed in March 1944 and served in Normandy, annihilated in the Falaise sack and later rebuilt in September in Köln-Wahn. It fought again in Arnhem and Amersfoot and in February 1945 in the Battle of Reichswald. As in many other armoured units, there were also several aces among the StuG commanders! The most incredible score of triumphs by a StuG was that of Oberwachtmeister Kurt Pfreundtne. With his Ausf.F Stug. Abt.244 at Stalingrad in early September 1942, he achieved the epic feat of destroying nine Soviet tanks in 20 minutes, which earned him the Knight's Cross. Wachtmeister Kurt Kirchner (Stug.Abt.667) managed to destroy 30 Soviet tanks in a few days in February 1942. Hauptmann Peter Franz, with his StuG from Abt. "Grossdeutschland", destroyed as many as 43 T-34/76 in the Battle of Borissovka in March 1943, also earning him the Ritter Kreuz! Finally, we would like to point out the claim of Waffen SS ace Walter Kniep of the 2nd StuG.Abt., 2nd SS Panzer Division 'Das Reich', who speaks of as many as 129 Soviet tanks for his unit between July and December 1943.

- **Kingdom of Romania:** received a hundred StuGs supplied by Germany and (post-war) even the USSR, designated *TA* or *TA T-3*. All German equipment was removed from service in 1950 and finally scrapped four years later due to the army's decision to use only Soviet armour.

- **Kingdom Bulgaria**: like the Romanians, Bulgaria also received many vehicles from Germany and (post-war) the USSR. Bulgaria, however, did not use any StuGs against the Soviets, the country having ended its alliance with Germany. switching to the Allies' side before the Soviets invaded. After the Second World War, these were used for a short period before being turned into fixed positions on the Krali Marko line on the border with neighbouring Turkey.

- **Finland:** 30 StuGs, nicknamed '*Sturmi*' by the Finns, were purchased in 1943 and another 29 in 1944, all directly from Germany. They were all used during the war against the Soviet Union in 1944. The first batch in 1943 destroyed at least eighty-seven enemy tanks against a loss of only eight StuGs. The last batch of 1944 was much less operational. After the war, the StuGs remained the main combat vehicles of the Finnish Army until the early 1960s, when they were phased out.

- **Czechoslovakia:** many vehicles were captured or detained after the war and later scrapped or sold to Syria. One vehicle is still preserved and is on display in Banská Bystrica, Slovakia.

- **France**: many were captured on French soil and after the war operated briefly before being scrapped or sold to Syria.

- **Hungarian kingdom:** 50 StuGs were donated by Germany in 1944. Hungary deployed its StuG IIIs against Soviet forces when they invaded the country from late 1944 until early 1945.

▲ ▼ Russian Campaign, two columns of early StuG III, around 1941/1942. Bundesarchiv (author's colouring).

- **Kingdom of Italy**: 12 vehicles were received from Germany in 1943. In Italy, the Sturmgeschütz was highly valued by the crews engaged against Allied armoured vehicles, but was dogged by constant break-downs, especially of the drive units. Italy received, in addition to the StuGs previously owned by local German units in 1943, a total of 12 Panzer III Ausf.Ns, 12 Panzer IV Ausf.Gs and 24 Flak 37 8.8 cm complete with half-tracks, to the Armoured Division 'M', which was destined for elite units composed of Blackshirts. With the fall of the fascist regime and the Italian armistice, all the equipment donated to them was recovered by the Germans and used again against the Allies.

 - **Norway:** German military equipment delivered as war damage, including several StuGs was used from 1947 to 1951.

- **Spain**: in 1943, Francoist Spain received 10 units as a sign of friendship and used them until 1954. They were later sold to Syria between 1950 and 1960. One Ausf. G of these is still in drivable condition in the Museo Histórico Militar de Cartagena, Spain.

- **Sweden**: they were equipped with an Ausf. D received from Denmark at the end of 1945 and used for trials and tests of anti-tank mines, and a variant Ausf. G used for spare parts.

- **Syria**: at least 30 half and possibly more obtained from various states including the Soviet Union, France, Spain and Czechoslovakia in the 1950s and beyond. They also ended up deployed in the water war against Israel in the mid-1960s, and also during the Six Day War in 1967, during which many of them were destroyed, or stripped for spare parts and partly relocated to the Golan Heights as forts. Some even remained in service in the 1973 Yom Kippur War! No doubt, an enormous longevity for this vehicle. Some former Syrian StuG IIIs that ended up in Israeli hands became monuments.

- **Soviet Union:** several hundred vehicles captured and then used for testing and modifications, including the SU-76i assault gun and the SG-122 self-propelled howitzer.

- **Yugoslavia:** StuG IIIs were also given to the pro-German Croatian Ustaše militia, most of which were captured in Yugoslavia by Tito's Yugoslav partisans during and after the war, as were all other vehicles op-erated by the Germans. These were used by the Yugoslav People's Army until the 1950s, when they were replaced by more modern combat vehicles.

▲ Interesting picture taken in Russia in 1943 showing a Hummel panzerhaubitze next to a Stug III ausf G.. Bundesarchiv (author's colouring).

▲ Detailed image of a Stug III ausf G destroyed in Normandy by a terrible internal explosion, France 1944 NARA (author's colouring).

▼ A Stug III ausf G put out of action on a road near the Gothic Line in Italy. 19 September 1944. NARA.

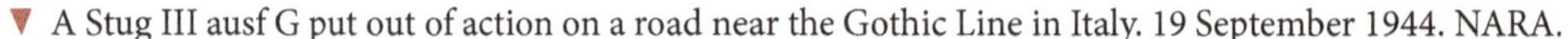

STURMGESCHÜTZ III Sd.Kfz. 142

STUG III AUSF G ASSAULT GUN, POLAND 1945

▲ StuG.III Ausf.G, in winter camouflage of an unidentified unit in Poland in March 1945.

DATA SHEET

	Ausf. A–B	Ausf. C-D	Ausf. E	Ausf. F	Ausf. G	StuH 42
General features						
Overall Dimensions						
Weight	20,7 t	20,7 t	22 t	23,3 t	22,9 t	24 t
Length	5,38 m	5,38 m	5,38 m	5,38 m	5,38 m	5,59 m
Width	2,92 m	2,92 m	2,92 m	2,92 m	2,92 m	2,95
Height	1,95 m	1,95 m	1,95 m	1,95 m	1,95 m	2,51 m
Armament						
Armament	7,5 L/24	7,5 L/24	7,5 L/24	7,5 L/43 o 48	7,5 Stuk 40 L/ 48	leFH 18
Secondary Arm.	=	=	1× MG 34	1× MG 34	2× MG 34	1× MG 34
Calibre	75mm	75mm	75mm	75mm	75mm	105mm
Elevation	-10° a +20°	-10° a +20°	-10° a +20°	-10° a +20°	-10° a +20°	-10° a +20°
Crew	4	4	4	4	4	4
Armour						
Front hull	15/50 mm	15/50 mm	50/80 mm	80 mm	90 mm	80+30mm
Vehicle average	10/50mm	10/50mm	15/80mm	30/80mm	60mm	30/50mm
Mobility						
Engine (Maybach)	HL 120 TRM 265 hp	HL 120 TRM 265 hp	HL 120 TRM 265 hp	HL 120 TRM 265 hp	HL 120 TRM V-12 300 hp	HL 120 TRM V-12 300 hp
Minimum Speed	20 km/h	20 km/h	20 km/h	20 km/h	25 km/h	24 km/h
Max. speed	40 km/h	40 km/h	40 km/h	40 km/h	40 km/h	40 km/h
Autonomy	160 km (road) 100 (general)	160 km (on road) 100 (general)	160 km (road) 100 (general)	140 km (road) 85 (general)	155 km (road) 100 (general)	170 km (road) 90 (general)
Total vehicles	36A+300B	50C+150D	284	366	9.400	1.300

▲ Well-known picture of a Stug of the Grossdeutschland division full of grenadieren! Russia, July 1943. Bundesarchiv (author's colouring).

STURMGESCHÜTZ III Sd.Kfz. 142

STUG III AUSF G ASSAULT GUN, GERMANY 1945

▲ StuG.III Ausf.G of an unidentified unit in Germany in early 1945.

▲ In 1942 a German unit of 10 StuG.III was temporarily subordinated to the 1st Armoured Field Division. In June 1944, the 2nd Armoured Division's losses were compensated for with 10 long-barrelled (L/48) StuG.IIIG assault guns in Galicia. The Hungarian military also received 40 StuG.IIIG assault guns which were used to equip the 7th Assault Gun Battalion in August 1944. (Péter Mujzer collection)

▼ Two Stug III ausf G assault guns knocked out by Allied bombing raids at Modrath, Germany. NARA.

STUH 42 ASSAULT GUN SD.KFZ. 142/2, ITALY 1945

▲ StuH.42 Sd.Kfz. 142/2, vehicle used in the last months of the war in the defence of the Italian lines, Italy, March 1945.

STUH 42 SD.KFZ. 142/2 ASSAULT GUN, RUSSIA 1943

▲ StuH.42 Sd.Kfz. 142/2. this tank appears here in the livery used in Russia during 1943 with only the balkenkreuz on its flanks for reinforcement, was the last evolution of the Stug III G.

STUH 42 SD.KFZ. 142/2 ASSAULT GUN, GERMANY 1945

▲ StuH 42 sd.kfz. 142/2. The same tank as on the previous page, but here in a camouflage version and without the lateral reinforcement skirts Germany 1945.

BIBLIOGRAPHY

- Peter Chamberlain, Hilary Doyle e Thomas L. Jentz, *Encyclopedia of German Tanks of World War Two Revised edition*, Londra, Arms & Armour Press, 1993, ISBN 1-85409-214-6.
- George Forty, *World War Two Tanks*, Osprey, 1995, ISBN 978-1-85532-532-6.
- Mueller, Peter; Zimmermann, Wolfgang. *Sturmgeschütz III - Backbone of the German Infantry.* 2008.
- Walter J. Spielberger. *Sturmgeschütz & Its variants* - Schiffer Publishing .
- Scafes, Cornel I; Scafes, Ioan I; Serbanescu, Horia Vl (2005). *Trupele Blindate din Armata Romana 1919-1947.* Bucuresti: Editura Oscar Print.
- Robert Michulec, *Armor battles on the Eastern Front (1)*,Hong Kong, Concord pub.company.
- Wolfgang Fleischer: *Die deutschen Sturmgeschütze 1935–1945.* Podzun-Pallas Verlag, 1996.
- Wolfgang Fleischer: *Waffen-Arsenal – Deutsche Sturmgeschütze im Einsatz. Band 176.* Podzun-Pallas Verlag.
- Frank Schulz: *Sturmgeschütz III Ausf. G – Privatsammlung J. Littlefield –* Photofile. NMC Nürnberg 2003.
- Dennis Oliver *Stug III & Stug IV: German Army, And Waffen-SS And Luftwaffe Western Front, 1944-1945* 2019.
- Steven J. Zaloga e Richard Chasemore *T-34 vs StuG III: Finland 1944* Osprey 2019.
- Dennis Oliver *Tank Craft 44 Stug III & Stug IV Assault Gun: German Army, Waffen-SS and Luftwaffe Units Eastern Front, 1944,* 2024.
- Dennis Oliver *Stug Assault Gun in the east Bagration to Berlin vol I.* Firefly coll. 2 2014.
- Dennis Oliver *Stug Assault Gun in the east Bagration to Berlin vol II.* Firefly coll. 7 2014.
- David Doyle *Sturmgeschütz: Germany's WWII Assault Gun (StuG): The Late War Versions: Germany's WWII Assault Gun (StuG), Vol.1 e 2: The Late War Versions* 2018
- Ben Hanvey *Sturmgeschütz: The StuG III Assault Gun (Rapid Reads)* 2015.
- Hilary L. Doyle *The Stug III Assault Gun, 1940-42* Osprey new vanguard 1996.
- Frank de Sisto *German sturmartillerie at war vol. 1.* Concord Pubblication 2008.
- Fulvio Miglia, *Le armi del Terzo Reich, il Panzerkampfwagen III*, Roma, Bizzarri, 1974.
- Frido Maria von Senger und Etterlin, *Die deutschen Panzer 1926-1945*, Bernard & Graefe Verlag, 1973.
- Janusz Ledwoch *Sturmgeschütz III.* Wydawnictwo Militaria Varsavia 1993
- Green, Michael; Anderson, Thomas; Schultz, Frank. *German Tanks of World War II. London, UK: Zenith Imprints. ISBN 9781610607209.*
- Maciej Noszcak *Sturmgeschütz III: A, B, F, F L43, F/8, G* (TopDrawings) Kagero 2020
- Vyacheslav Kozitsyn *Sturmgeschütz III & Sturmhaubitze 42* (Ostfront Warfare Series) 2019
- George Forty *Die deutsche Panzerwaffe im Zweiten Weltkrieg.* Bechtermünz, Augsburg 1998, ISBN 3-8289-5327-1.
- Steven Zaloga M10 Tank Destroyer vs StuG III Assault Gun: Germany 1944 (Duel Book 53) Opsrey
- Alexander Lüdeke *Panzer der Wehrmacht 1933-1945.* 3. Auflage, Motorbuch-Verlag, Stuttgart 2010, ISBN 978-3-613-02953-8.
- Ferdinand Maria von Senger und Etterlin *Die deutschen Panzer 1926–1945.* Bernard & Graefe, Bonn 1998, ISBN 3-7637-5988-3.
- Jan Suermond *Wehrmacht-Fahrzeuge - Restaurierte Rad- und Ketten-Kfz. 1. Auflage.* Motorbuch Verlag, Stuttgart 2005, ISBN 3-613-02513-2.

TITLES ALREADY PUBLISHED

TWE-021 EN

www.ingramcontent.com/pod-product-compliance
Lightning Source LLC
Chambersburg PA
CBHW041816110726
48006CB00019B/2405